Simple Man's Leadership Guide

Simple Leadership Tips For A Complicated World

Reginald Hairston

I have been blessed to gain a wealth of leadership knowledge from the leaders I've come into contact with over time. Experience has to some degree converted the knowledge gained into my personal toolbox of wisdom for which I am forever grateful. Chief among all of these influencers is my grandfather, George Alex King. A man born in 1915 and raised under the oppressive weight of segregation, he chose to put all of energy into raising his family. He once said to me, "I had an opportunity to go to Japan to take a job, but I decided it was a man's job to stay with and raise his family." To this day, I cannot quantify the positive impact that viewpoint has had on my interaction with my family. Through him, I learned to see individuals through the prism of their life experiences, to understand that life experiences create wise men and women, and to understand that tapping into their treasure trove of wisdom should be actively pursued by anyone who purports to being a life-long learner. To this day, my grandfather, a man who never had the chance to advance beyond the third grade is still the wisest man I've ever known.

I also thank my wife Tracey for 25 years of love and patience, and my children, Lauren, Naomi, and Miles for the joy and purpose they bring to my life, my mother (Carolyn Williams) for bringing me up "the right way", and my best friend (Julius Reynolds II) for always having my back. Above all, I thank God for his continuing grace and mercy.

Contents

Introduction

Leaders should actively work to improve their skills as leaders of people and organizations. This Guide attempts to give each reader a series of points that can be used to assess themselves. In some cases, it will be helpful to write key points down, and then take time to evaluate the points over a period of time. Bottom-line, this Guide wants to make you an active reader focused on achieving real positive growth in your evolution as a leader. Although it may sound presumptuous to assume this Guide can help you improve, I believe the Guide will do just that, if you are serious about improving. The change may occur because you agree with some or all of what is said or it may happen because you disagree and subsequently take time to figure out what works for you. In either case, you must take an active role towards improvement. As you navigate through this Guide, please take time to write down your thoughts. In fact, most sections have questions for you to consider. The thoughts you write down will form the baseline from which you will gauge yourself and will help you gain a better sense for how others perceive you. Everyone who takes a serious interest in change understands that it doesn't occur overnight, so periodically you need to check back to see what you wrote in the past, in order to see how far you have evolved. Good luck!

Are Leaders Born or Made?

If you ask the following questions to 1000 people, you will likely find that opinions are equally split:

1. Are leaders born?
2. Are leaders made?

What do you think? Before moving on with this Guide, take a moment to evaluate why you believe the way you do. Write your thoughts down and if you have time, discuss them with a friend, spouse, co-worker or mentor. Your answer and understanding of the answers will form the foundation for how much value you will or can gain from this book. When you have completed this first task, turn the page and explore the areas highlighted throughout this book as critical areas to concentrate your efforts. By no means is the list exhaustive; but the focus areas will hopefully serve as good points of reference regardless of where you find yourself on the leadership continuum. In addition, there are a multitude of best sellers that deal specifically with becoming a good and effective leader such as:

1. The 21 Irrefutable Laws of Leadership: Follow Them and People Will Follow You (10th Anniversary Edition) – John Maxwell

2. Leadership: In Turbulent Times - Doris Kearns Goodwin

3. Leaders Eat Last: Why Some Teams Pull Together and Others Don't – Simon Sinek

4. Management Mess to Leadership Success: 30 Challenges to Become the Leader You Would Follow - Scott Jeffrey Miller

Be Yourself!

Simple right? If it's simple, why do so many self-proclaimed leaders have such a hard time with this one? More than 28 years ago, I found myself in a situation where a Marine Corps Gunnery Sergeant and I were headed for a confrontation. To say I was a little concerned was an understatement. My concern lay in the fact that I, a Second Lieutenant for less than a year, found myself in a situation where I needed to influence the Gunnery Sergeant to comply with the instructions he had been given.

For those of you who have never served in the military, just picture a brand-new inexperienced supervisor confronting a seasoned employee. When I looked at the Gunnery Sergeant, I saw a man who had been serving in the Marine Corps back when I was still in elementary. Couple this with the societal images of a hard-core Marine and you may start to get a picture of why I was concerned. Bottom-line, if he refused to do what I told him, then what? Stuck in this conundrum, I approached my Colonel (Chief Operating Officer), told him the situation, and asked him if I should yell at the Gunnery Sergeant or simply have a conversation? The answer the Colonel gave was simple and formed the foundation for how I have dealt with people ever since. The Colonel told me to be myself!

Specifically, he said, "Be yourself and not what you think the Gunnery Sergeant expects you to be. If you are not a yeller, don't yell because it will come across as phony and the Gunnery Sergeant will not respect you." Well, I had the conservation with the Gunnery Sergeant, and I'm proud to say that I did not raise my voice. Unfortunately for the Gunnery Sergeant, he raised his voice and promptly got called into the Colonel's office for a good old-fashioned butt chewing. Although, the Colonel essentially solved my first problem, his advice was instrumental to shaping my approach for dealing with individuals from that point on.

How about you, do you know yourself? Take some time to get

to know yourself by writing down and answering these simple questions:

1. Are you an extrovert or an introvert?

2. Do you like being around the people you work with and more importantly the people who work for you?

3. What are your strengths?

4. What are your weaknesses?

5. What three things do you wish you could change about yourself?

Once you answer the above questions, share your answers with three people, preferably you will pick more than just your closest friends, and ask them to write down their opinions of you. Focus on the following questions:

1. What are my strengths?

2. What are my weaknesses?

3. What three things would you like me to change?

Now, I have to caution you that you may not like the answers. However, the goal is to see how close your opinion of yourself comes to matching the opinion of what others think of you. Once you complete this exercise, it is completely up to you what you do with the information but I highly encourage you to think deeply about the results and then assess how to improve. The first step in making positive changes is the realization that change is inevitable. If you haven't done so already, take time to read, "Who Moved My Cheese." As you begin to understand the characters within the book, try to determine which one is the most like you. After reading the book numerous times, I finally came to the conclusion, that at different points in my life, my behavior has resembled all of the main characters.

Set a Positive Example

I'd rather see a sermon than hear one any day; I'd rather one should walk with me than merely tell the way. The eye is a better pupil, more willing than the ear; Fine counsel is confusing, but example is always clear, And the best of all the preachers are the men who live their creeds, for to see a good put in action is what everybody needs... -- Edgar A. Guest

What does it mean to set a positive example? Setting a positive example is as easy as visually doing in front of others what you expect them to do. It could be as simple as arriving to work on or before the start time, saying good morning or hello to everyone you see throughout the day, taking great caution to maintain an even temperament, even when you are mad, taking time to ask someone how they are doing and then listening to the answer. As easy as it is, it is also difficult! What about the days when you don't feel like speaking to everyone? What do you do when you want to hit the snooze button one more time, even if it means you will be five minutes late for work or an appointment?

What if you know someone needs to talk, but you don't feel like listening? There are too many scenarios or potential situations to name, so suffice it to say that as the leader, you are never free from the spotlight. However, you are still human and your people will understand as long as you are genuine and caring. Once your people know you care about them, most of them will bend over backwards to care about you. To help foster a good working environment, consider publishing a work place philosophy that outlines your expectations for your employees and gives them a roadmap into what they can expect from you.

Care About Your People

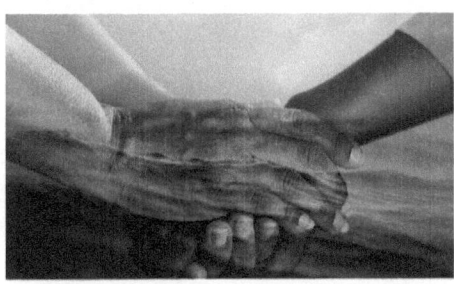 Do you care about your people? At this stage, I want you to take time to evaluate what's important to you and honestly assess where people fall out on your list. The one thing you cannot do is trick people into thinking you care, so for your sake, be honest with yourself. Everyone who comes in contact with you naturally sizes you up and makes an assessment of your ability to relate to them as an individual. The assessment may be incorrect, in your opinion, but for the assessor it is accurate. Now, this is just one person's opinion, but I believe it is in your best interest to take time to get to know your folks and to take interest in what matters to them.

If you give the impression you don't care, you can best believe your folks won't care about you. So how do you show interest? From my vantage point, a real leader pursues the art of caring to the point it becomes second nature, but realizes that caring doesn't equate to letting your people have their way all the time. A caring leader seeks to understand his or her people, and you do this by taking time to get to know them.

The more people you have in your organization, the harder it gets to know everyone. This is okay! You need to identify your key influencers (the individuals who carry your message). Get to know them, and then expect them to get to know the people they are responsible for. If done correctly, your key influencers will help build a community of motivated workers, soldiers, executives, etc.

Always remember that employees don't care how much you know until they know how much you care! I heard this from numerous leaders over the years and recently discovered that the quote comes from our Theodore Roosevelt. Time and experience have taught me that the the words are true. Make no mistake, you can't talk people into believing you care about them; they will make that determination on their own by observing your day to day actions.

Open Communication

"The burden of communication is on the communicator not the communicatee!" I was a young Captain of Marines (supervisor) the first time I heard this, and quite frankly, it made me mad. It made me mad because my boss was telling me that it was my fault the sergeant (junior employee) didn't understand my expectations. When I finally calmed down enough to consider what my boss meant, I realized he was right. Not only was he right, the lesson learned on that day shaped all communications I've had with juniors, peers, seniors, my wife, kids, friends, and associates to this day. Okay, so what does it mean when I say the, "The burden of communication is on the communicator not the communicatee?" Think about it, have you ever told someone to do something and even though they did exactly what you said, it was completely the wrong thing to do. Undoubtedly, you probably said, "I told you to do …" To which the person replied, "I did!" Now you tell me, whose fault is it that what you requested could be interpreted in more than one-way? Once you break the habit of trying to fix blame on others, you will begin to see major improvements in your ability to think through what you are going to say, verbally and in writing. Your ability to improve in this area or accept responsibility in this area will correlate directly to the trust others have in your ability to lead.

Acknowledge Excellence

Bottom-line – when an individual or a team consistently excels, acknowledge them in public. It could be in the form of a verbal compliment, a monetary award, time off, etc. Once you acknowledge excellence, it breeds more excellence. I want you to practice giving subtle compliments and praise to your folks. I promise you will be pleased with the long- term results. Your assignment is to write down all the ways in which you can award hard work. Whether it be through a Letter of Appreciation or a monetary award, knowing what's available makes it easier to determine the right level of recognition, when needed. If your organization doesn't have good written recognition policies, consider writing them yourself.

Fair Treatment, Individual Differences

It is amazing how much the idea of treating people fairly causes problems for so many leaders. I'm going to keep this one as simple and short as possible.

Bottom-line: Establish the same set of expectations/business rules for everyone. I recommend publishing a work place philosophy.

1. Get to know your people.

2. Accept the fact that everyone learns differently. Don't assume everyone knows you care about them, make sure they know you care. "People don't care how much you know until they know how much you care!"

3. Perform written, honest counseling on everyone, including difficult employees. The best time to do a non-confrontational counseling is prior to an incident, so do yourself a favor and lay out your expectations at the beginning of the employer/employee relationship. From this point, you can conduct periodic follow-up counseling's to ensure everyone has a common understanding of what's expected/tolerated/required.

4. Enforce the company / organization rules.

Have you ever been in a situation where you were accused of being unfair?
1. What did you do wrong? Probably nothing right (smile).

2. Okay, if you didn't do anything wrong, what was perceived by others as being wrong? Remember, this is for your growth so be honest.

3. How did you get through the situation?

4. What will you do different in the future?

If you are unable to think of a time when you were perceived as being the bad guy or girl, think of a time when you perceived that someone treated you unfairly. Now assume the unfair treatment was not done consciously, what could the offender have done differently? What could you have done differently?

Guard Against the Perception of Favoritism

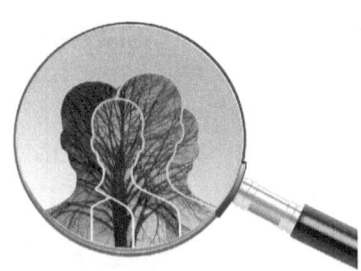

Guarding against the perception of favoritism is actually more difficult than it sounds. The reason is simple – you are being evaluated every time you interact with your personnel. As a part of this evaluation, your employees pay attention to everything you do or don't do. Your challenge is to remain consistent even though the situation and people you deal with are diverse. To be quite honest, I'm not sure if it's completely possible to avoid this one, but understanding that it is a situation you should be constantly aware of places you ahead of the game.

1. Have you ever worked for someone who clearly favored individuals?

2. How did it make you feel?

3. What did the experience teach you?

Maybe you already show favoritism and didn't realize it until now. What do you do now?

Rank your employees and then define why you ranked them where you did (this is for your eyes only, so don't place this on social media).

Note – the goal is not to change how you feel about your personnel, it's to make you aware that you may be inadvertently favoring some employees. Remember, your actions are always under a microscope.

Manage Priorities

On any given day we start the day with a mental list of the things to be accomplished. Isn't it frustrating when we don't get them accomplished? In more cases than not, it comes down to a mismanagement of priorities. If you take a moment to prioritize your tasks, the job of completing the tasks becomes more manageable. In those cases when you can't finish everything, you will at least feel better that you accomplished the most important tasks. So, imagine, if you can't manage your personal priorities, how do you prioritize the tasks of your small business, corporation, military organization, etc.?

- Challenge 1: write down the tasks you wish to accomplish and through the course of one month, track your progress or the work of your employees. As the month progresses, you will undoubtedly have to re-prioritize some tasks, but don't become discouraged, this is natural and expected.

- Challenge 2: Require your employees to do the same thing. At the end of the month, conduct some mentoring sessions to get a sense for how it worked.

Set Realistic Expectations

Here is an area I failed in miserably when I was first starting out. In my exuberance, I thought I could change everything and everybody for the better. Arrogant right? It wasn't until I realized that most of us are simply building solid foundations, in incremental steps. In most cases, it is difficult to fully understand the future goodness of your actions, assuming your actions are meant for good. So, here is the challenge:

1. Figure out what you wish to accomplish.

2. Create a mental or written plan for accomplishing the mission or reaching your objectives.

3. Set realistic milestones for achieving the mission/objectives.

This is easier said than done. What if your goal is to change the underlying climate of your organization from one of low morale to one of high morale? How do you go about doing it? How do you know when you have achieved your goal? How do you ensure you are not just seeing what you want to see? The short answer is time. Time is the measuring rod by which all actions or lack thereof are measured. It takes time to gain trust, time to get to know your people, time to learn the art of personal communication, etc. Take a look at the organization you are in now and determine what you wish to fix. Is the fix within your ability to influence? If it is, what's your plan? Write the plan down and track your progress. Accept the reality that in some cases you are laying the foundation of success for your successor. Remember - don't be afraid to modify the plan. Your ability to adjust may result in an improved bottom-line.

Make Timely Decisions

A leader seldom has time to gather all the information needed to make a perfect decision, so don't waste time waiting on information that may never come. I'm sure you've heard the saying, "An 80% plan executed now is better than a 100% plan executed too late." It is perfectly okay to make sound judgments with the available information on hand and then adjust, if needed, as more information is provided. Your job is to continuously prepare for those times when you have to make the hard decisions, and hard decisions are rarely ever fully informed by all the relevant information. The best leaders thrive on the pressure of making the hard calls and actively learn from the outcome of those decisions.

1. When you make the right decision, heap praise on others.

2. When you make a bad call, accept the blame without trying to make excuses. Excuses are for the incompetent. Now, I want you to think of a time when you waited too long to make a decision.

a. Why did you hesitate?

b. What did you learn from that experience?

c. Think of a time when you made a good decision. Did you praise the folks who advised you or did you take all the credit? How do you think it made the folks around you feel?

Don't Be Afraid to Modify a Decision

This goes hand in hand with the making of timely decisions. The only thing worse than making a bad decision is the failure to correct that decision, when you realize there is a better way. I have found that in more cases than not, the leader who refuses to adjust does so out of embarrassment. I know you've seen it. Someone makes a decision, realizes the decision doesn't make sense, realizes that everyone else understands the folly of the decision, but stubbornly refuses to adjust. It's almost as if the person is saying, "I must show that I believed in the decision and changing it will make me look weak." I have news for you; the courage to modify/change your mind is the sign of a conscientious and strong leader.

1. Have you ever allowed your pride to stand in the way of changing a decision? If yes, write that situation down and dissect it.

2. What, if anything would you do differently? Why?

Minimize Dissension

I wish I had a magic formula to share that would ensure all your employees, soldiers, sailors, Marines, Coasties or Airmen would agree with all your decisions and that there would never be friction in the workplace. Luckily, I don't. In reality, you will find that a healthy dose of dissension is good for an organization. In other words, you don't want to be surrounded by people who always say yes, even when the answer should be no. At the same time, you don't want an environment that fosters second-guessing once a decision has been made.

Things to consider:

1. Seek counsel/advice before making controversial decisions (if time allows).

2. Present your vision/idea to the key communities within your organization. This could be the floor supervisor in a plant/company or the senior enlisted member in a military organization. The goal is to identify the friction points early. This is also an opportunity to get the key players to support the decision whether they like it or not.

3. Specifically ask each member of your command/organization to commit to making your decision successful. It is easier to tell folks they don't have a say in the decisions being made, but it is healthier for the organization to make your folks a part of the decision-making process, when time allows.

Once again, the size of the organization is the driver. However, regardless of organizational size, there are always key influencers. Don't fail to consult with or back-brief your key influencers. Once a decision is made, make sure your key influencers understand the importance of backing the decision regardless of their personal views. They will do this as long as they understand that you will make corrections as needed.

Compromise to Win

Now, this is going to be a difficult one for most of you! How in the world can you compromise and still win? Imagine this scenario:

Every day, James came to work full of enthusiasm and with big ideas about how to improve the business. James' employer was a very focused individual with a keen sense of where he wanted to take the business and was reluctant to allow anyone the opportunity for free thought or expression. Now, James was by far the best worker and his dedication to job was the primary reason the employer's business was thriving. A couple of years passed and James grew weary with the fact his voice was never heard. Finally, he decided to take his talents elsewhere. After departing the business, the employer's business declined and before long the employer had to close the business.

Now, imagine for an instant that James approached his employer with one of his great ideas. Imagine even further that the employer was not completely convinced the idea would work; in fact, the employer was reluctant to try something new, but he allowed James to implement the idea and see it through. For the sake of argument, assume that James' idea caused the business to thrive in a way the employer could never have imagined. This is a clear case of compromising to win. The employer allowed James to have his way in spite of his reservation and James' enthusiasm was re-kindled. As a result of allowing James to take some control, James went on to improve the business and eventually became a business partner. The final outcome was by compromising to win, the employer's overall business won, even though he took a reluctant chance on the front end!

Think about what it means to compromise in order to win. In the above scenario, the employer didn't actually lose anything but the need to be in full control.

Be Seen

I'm not going to expound too much on this one. Let me just say that you should never under-estimate the value of your physical presence. Now, this assumes your people don't hate you because you are a poor leader. At least once a day, I recommend that you take time to at least say good morning to the folks around you. If you are in a large organization it becomes impractical to get around to everyone, but you best believe that the word of you being a person who is easy to talk to or not will get around. Get out from behind your desk, take time to talk to your people and continuously reinforce your core beliefs. It has been said that employees take on the characteristics of their employer. I've found this to be true in military organizations because members buy into the espirit de corps. I imagine the same holds true for small businesses. In any case, it is incumbent upon you to shape your organization.

Supervise

The most important thing you can do is supervise. Do not mistake the importance of supervision with micromanagement. For the record, I am strongly against micromanaging because it sends the wrong message to your folks. Supervising allows you to acknowledge excellence, provide corrective direction and get feedback from your employees. In order to supervise, you need to understand the end state you are trying to obtain and the role of your employees in reaching that end state. I personally believe that clear guidance (communication) coupled with a sincere show of trust in your team's abilities will normally lead to results that surpass your expectations. Micromanagement on the other hands tends to send the message that we don't trust our employees and lends itself to minimal effort on the part of the employees.

Self-Evaluate

Arguably the most important step on your journey to improve as a leader is this step. Everyone goes through some level of self-evaluation, but I believe it is rarely helpful. It is rarely helpful because we tend to be easier on ourselves than we are on others. However, real change can only occur when we are presented with an honest picture of who and what we are as leaders. I challenge you to take every step outlined in this book and rate your performance against them. Once you become accustomed to taking a realistic look at yourself, you can make conscious decisions about what you need to change. Believe me, it's not easy. Years ago, I was told I didn't listen well and I completely rejected it. It wasn't until I faced this reality that I was able to improve my listening skills. This small change coupled with the belief that I bear the responsibility for clearly communicating to my employees is the foundation upon which my leadership style is built. What is your foundation?

Conclusion

Hopefully you found something in this Guide that will prove useful as you continue your journey as a leader. I humbly thank every soul that touched my life in either a positive or negative manner because I learned from all of them. Remember, the outlined steps in this book worked for me, but may not work for you. When it's all said and done, we all must find what works for us as individuals. Good luck!!!

About The Author

Reginald Hairston

Reginald Hairston is a retired Marine Corps Colonel with a deep passion for teaching young leaders how to lead.

Books By This Author

Military Retirement Primer: The Little Things You Need To Know Now

Retiring from the military is challenging and for a good deal of future retirees, the volume of information you are expected to absorb is overwhelming. This eBook attempts to clear up some of the confusion associated with the transition, and instead of trying to give the reader massive amounts of information, the focus of effort is on subjects that matter the most to retirees.